*A gift for*

*From*

# A Mother's Heart Knows

## MARGARET McSWEENEY

# A Mother's Heart Knows

Published by J. Countryman, a division of Thomas Nelson, Inc,
Nashville, Tennessee 37214.

Project editor, Terri Gibbs

Designed by Left Coast Design, Portland, Oregon.

ISBN: 1-4041-0136-5

www.thomasnelson.com
www.jcountryman.com
www.margaretmcsweeney.com

Printed and bound in China

*In loving memory of my mother,*

*Carolyn Rhea, whose heart blessed my*

*life and inspired me to follow Christ.*

A Mother's Heart Knows...

A mother's heart knows

in the still of the night.

A mother's heart knows
when her child is all right.

A mother's heart
knows when to
offer to guide.

A mother's heart knows

when to step to the side.

A mother's heart knows

how to face the rough years.

A mother's heart knows
how to chase away fears.

A mother's heart knows
comforting words to say.

A mother's heart knows
how to take time to pray.

A mother's heart knows
how to laugh and to live.

A mother's heart knows
to accept and forgive.

A mother's heart knows how
to sense a child's need.

A mother's heart knows
when to guard against greed.

A mother's heart knows how
to measure each word.

A mother's heart knows the
best thoughts to be heard.

A mother's heart knows

when to knock on the door.

A mother's heart knows
not to judge or keep score.

A mother's heart knows how
to reach out and share.

A mother's heart knows
how to teach and be fair.

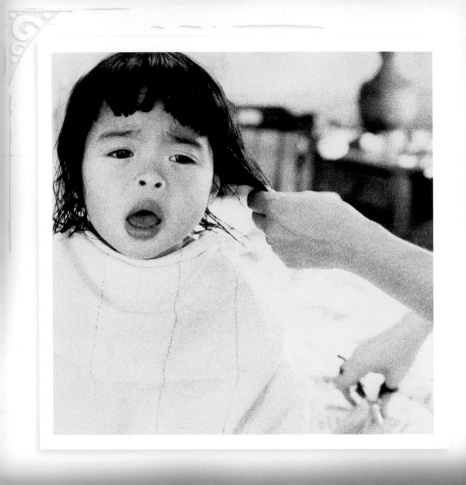

A mother's heart knows
to find value in strife.

A mother's heart knows how
to treasure each life.

A mother's heart knows
how to always rejoice.

A mother's heart knows where
to find that still voice.

A mother's heart knows
the importance of trust.

A mother's heart knows how

to seek what is just.

A mother's heart knows
to provide and protect.

A mother's heart knows

to listen and respect.

A mother's heart knows and
wants to understand.

A mother's
heart knows
when to hold
her child's
hand.

A mother's heart knows

how to answer each call.

A mother's heart knows

how to soften a fall.

A mother's heart knows how
to stretch and to grow.

A mother's heart knows

when it's time to let go.

A mother's heart knows the
real meaning of love.

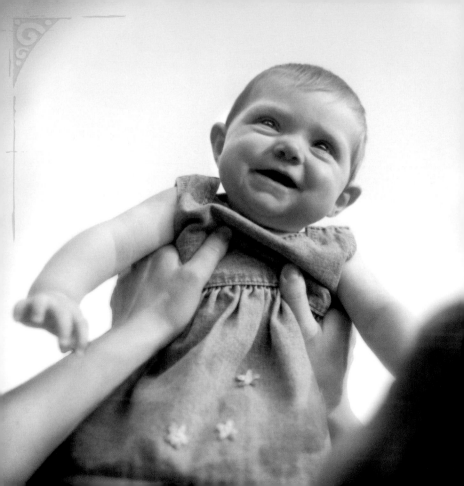

A mother's heart knows her
child comes from above.